REMEMBERING

The Journey Back to the Pre-Conditioned Self

You were never broken. You simply forgot.

Mardoche Sidor, MD
Karen Dubin, PhD, LCSW
SWEET Institute

SWEET Institute Publishing
Transformational Books for a Transformational World

Published by:

SWEET Institute Publishing

New York, NY

WWW.SWEETInstitutePublishing.com

First Edition

Printed in the United States of America

ISBN (Paperback): [978-1-968105-03-7]

Cover Design: [SWEET Institute Publishing]

Interior Design and Layout: [SWEET Institute Publishing]

For bulk orders, permissions, or media inquiries, please contact:

info@sweetinstitutepublishing.com

SWEET Institute Publishing
Transformational Books for a Transformational World

Dedication

To the ones who were told they were too much,
too loud, too quiet, too broken,
too sensitive, too angry, too complicated,
too soft for this world—
and believed it.

To the ones who forgot how powerful they are.
To the ones who made it through anyway.
To the ones still trying to find their way back.
And to the ones who never left—
but waited, patiently, for the rest of us to remember.

This book is for you.

And for every clinician, healer, teacher, parent, leader, neighbor, and friend
who has chosen presence over performance,
curiosity over control,
and love over fear.

You are not just changing lives.
You are helping the world remember.

Thank you.

Other Books by Mardoche Sidor, M.D; Karen Dubin, PhD, LCSW; with the SWEET Institute

- Journey to Empowerment
- Discovering Your Worth: Everything You Need to Feel Fulfilled
- The Power of Faith: A Harvard-Trained Psychiatrist Speaking on Faith
- The Psychotherapy Certificate Course: The Clinician and Coach Manual (Books 1–3)
- The Anxiety Course: The Workbook
- What's Missing
- NLP for Clinicians
- 50 SWEET Poems: Reflections on life, love and self
- The Power of Belief: How Ideas Shape Leaders, Nations and the Future
- The Courage to Care: Stories of Healing, Hope, and the Power of Social Work: Told by Over 50 SWEET Institute Social Workers
- Transforming Team Relationships From the Inside Out

Table of Contents

Foreword 7

Preface 9

Introduction 11

Why This Book 13

What This Book Is About 14

How This Book Works 15

Who This Book Is For 17

How to Read This Book 18

Acknowledgments 19

Part I: The Paradigm Shift 20

CHAPTER 1: The Fallacy of Fixing 21

CHAPTER 2: The Pre-Conditioned Self 25

CHAPTER 3: The Four Layers of Transformation 30

Part II: The Four Layers in Depth 36

CHAPTER 4: Working at the Conscious Layer 37

CHAPTER 5: Entering the Preconscious 43

CHAPTER 6: Meeting the Unconscious 49

CHAPTER 7: The Existential Integration 54

Part III: Integration and Application 60

CHAPTER 8: The Practice of Remembering 61

CHAPTER 9: Remembering in Clinical Practice 66

CHAPTER 10: Systems That Forget 71

CHAPTER 11: Stories of Remembering 76

CHAPTER 12: The Revolution of Wholeness 80

Closing Poem: You Were Never Broken   84

Epilogue: You Were Always Enough   86

Conclusion: From Remembering to Living   88

Invitation to You, the Reader   90

Final Acknowledgments   92

The Reader Integration Toolkit   94

Appendices   99

Additional Resources by the Authors   104

About the Authors   107

Foreword

Dr. Jovanna Marc, Founder of MARC | Certified Peer Specialist

I remember what it felt like to be told I needed to be fixed.
The silence after trauma.
The labels that replaced my name.
The well-meaning professionals who never thought to ask, *"Who were you before the pain?"*

But I also remember the first time someone saw me—not as a diagnosis, but as a whole person.
A soul.
A story still unfolding.

That's the spirit of this book.

Remembering: The Journey Back to the Pre-Conditioned Self doesn't just speak to the mind—it speaks to the deeper self, the one beneath the scripts we were taught to survive. The one that existed before the conditioning, before the interruption, before our identities were rewritten by trauma.

This isn't a textbook.
It's an invitation.

An invitation into a sacred circle—where healing is not about symptom management, but about reclaiming dignity.
Where clinicians become mirrors, not mechanics.
Where people with lived experience are not passive recipients of care, but powerful participants in their own healing.

This book is for us.
It honors the parts of ourselves that were silenced, buried, or forgotten.
It offers not just a model of care, but a pathway back to our truth.

I've walked this path—from survival to remembering.
I've built programs and systems where this kind of remembering is possible.

And I can say with confidence: what you're holding is more than a book. It's a guide to transformation.

To every peer, clinician, healer, and leader reading these pages:
Let this book challenge how you've been taught to see others—and yourself.
Let it soften you. Let it awaken you. Let it bring you home to something true.

Because we are not here to be fixed.
We are here to be seen.
We are here to be held.
We are here to remember.

— Dr. Jovanna Marc

Founder, Multi Assistance Resource Center (MARC)
Certified Peer Specialist

Preface

By Mardoche Sidor, MD

I have sat across from thousands of people—patients, clinicians, staff, leaders, residents, survivors—and I have seen the same thing in all of them:
A flicker.
A pulse.
A presence that never stopped existing, even when everything else was stripped away.

And yet, so often, our systems do not see this. They see dysfunction. They see diagnosis. They see behavior that needs to be managed.

They rarely ask: Who was this person before the pain? Before the trauma? Before the conditioning?

That question has guided my life's work.
And this book is the answer.
I did not write this book because I needed to say something.
I wrote it because I couldn't stay silent any longer.

We are losing people. Not only to suicide, addiction, incarceration homelessness, and disconnection. We are losing people to the lie that they are broken.

And we are losing clinicians and caregivers to the lie that their job is to fix them. I don't believe that anymore. I haven't for a long time.

This book is about remembering.
Not remembering trauma—but remembering truth.
Not reprocessing pain—but returning to the self that existed before it.

What you're holding is not just a model. It is a movement.

A remembering of who we were before the world interrupted our wholeness.

The framework you will find here—the four layers of transformation: Conscious, Preconscious, Unconscious, and Existential—is not a theory.

It is a map. It is the path I've used as a psychiatrist, as a teacher, as a medical director, and as a human being.

It is the path I've walked with individuals who've been institutionalized for decades.
With clinicians who've burned out from helping everyone but themselves.
With children who stopped laughing too soon.

And with my own inner self, who—despite everything—never stopped reaching for light.

This book is for all of us.

If you've ever felt like healing was more than managing symptoms...
If you've ever suspected that your soul is still intact under the strategy...
If you've ever seen someone's wholeness flicker through their pain...

Then this book is already yours.

Use it. Share it. Live it. Do so, not perfectly, but intentionally. Do so, not as a script, but as a remembering. Because you were never broken. You simply forgot. And now...

You are ready to return.

With all my presence,

Mardoche Sidor, MD

Introduction

By Karen Dubin, PhD, LCSW

When we began writing this book, I didn't know how much of myself I would meet in its pages.

I've been a social worker, a supervisor, an educator, and a daughter of this system for almost three decades. I've sat in courts, jails, and therapy rooms, and I've walked side by side with my clients doing field work. I've written mitigation reports, evaluations, and treatment plans. I've taught ethics and burnout prevention and trauma theory. And still, nothing prepared me for the power of this shift—from fixing to remembering.

We live in a world that is constantly telling people what they are not; Not enough, Not ready, Not safe, or Not whole.

In clinical settings, we tell people they're resistant, non-compliant, or high-risk. We praise functionality and independence as if that's the same thing as freedom. We see symptoms, but not stories. We see behaviors, but not meaning. And, more importantly, we forget to ask the most important question of all: Who were you before the context you live in told you?

This book asks that question—and doesn't look away. It introduces a framework that has changed how I practice, how I teach, how I supervise, and how I live. The SWEET Topographical and Existential Model of Transformation moves us through four essential layers:

- The Conscious, where we begin with safety, behavior, and structure

- The Preconscious, where patterns and beliefs are revealed

- The Unconscious, where the body stores what the mind cannot speak

- And the Existential, where we remember that we are free, that we are responsible, and that we can choose again

We walk through each of these layers not with pathology, but with presence. Not with diagnosis, but with humanity. And as we do, we don't just change as individuals—we begin to change the systems we are part of.

This book will give you tools.

It will offer reflections, visuals, practices, scripts, and frameworks you can apply in your sessions, your supervision, your agency, your home. But more than that, it will invite you to remember:

- Who you were before the conditioning
- What it means to help someone return to themselves
- And what kind of world we could co-create if we stopped trying to fix people and started honoring their wholeness

This is book is designed to sit with, to practice with, and to come back to.

So however you arrived here, whether as a clinician, a peer, a student, a "survivor," a leader, or someone still figuring out who they are, welcome. You do not have to be more. You only have to remember.

Let's begin.

Karen Dubin, PhD, LCSW

Why This Book

Because people are not problems to be solved.

Because too many clinicians are burning out trying to fix what was never broken.

Because too many systems are still focused on behavior without understanding meaning.

Because trauma is not just personal—it's structural, generational, and systemic.

Because remembering is a healing act, a political act, and a spiritual act.

This book was born out of necessity.

From decades of work with individuals who were never seen beneath their symptoms.

From clinicians who were overworked, under-supported, and silently longing for a new way.

From systems that were created to help—but often forget the humanity at the center of the work.

This book was written because healing isn't linear, but it is layered.

And when we understand the layers, we remember how to come home.

What This Book Is About

This book introduces a new model of care, healing, and transformation called the Topographical and Existential Model of Remembering, developed by the SWEET Institute. It moves through four layers of transformation:

1. **The Conscious Layer** – where structure, behavior, and safety begin

2. **The Preconscious Layer** – where we uncover beliefs, schemas, and early messages

3. **The Unconscious Layer** – where we access the repressed and the symbolic

4. **The Existential Layer** – where meaning, choice, and identity are restored

This is a book for clinicians, coaches, educators, peer specialists, supervisors, parents, and anyone who supports others in their healing journey—or who is on that journey themselves.

It blends lived experience with scientific research. It combines narrative, dialogue, case reflections, and direct application. It teaches, reflects, challenges, and reorients—again and again—toward remembering.

It is a clinical model, a spiritual guide, a poetic map, and a quiet revolution.

How This Book Works

This book is not just something to read. It's something to use, to return to, to live with. It is structured around the SWEET Topographical and Existential Model of Transformation, which unfolds across four essential layers:

1. **Conscious** – behavior, routine, lifestyle, structure

2. **Preconscious** – beliefs, schemas, internalized narratives

3. **Unconscious** – repressed material, symbolic meaning, emotional truth

4. **Existential** – meaning, freedom, responsibility, identity

Each layer is explored through its own dedicated chapter, followed by chapters that integrate these layers into clinical practice, systems change, and personal transformation.

This book blends multiple modalities—CBT, ACT, Schema Therapy, Psychodynamic Therapy, Narrative Therapy, Existential Therapy, and more—into a unified, layered framework that helps people not just change behaviors, but remember who they were before they were shaped by fear, pain, and survival.

Chapter Structure

Every chapter includes:

- **Conversational Dialogue** – to ground the theme in human truth

- **Scientific Insight** – rooted in data, theory, and research

- **Charts and Visuals** – for clarity and deeper understanding

- **Tools and Practices** – so you can apply the content in real time

- **Commitment Practice** – to integrate the learning into daily life

- **Scientific References** – for further reading

Who This Book Is For

- Clinicians, supervisors, and program leaders
- Peer specialists and those with lived experience
- Educators, coaches, and community healers
- Individuals navigating their own healing journey
- Anyone working within systems that serve human beings

Whether you're here to apply this model in your practice, your agency, your family, or your life—you belong here.

Use It Personally or Professionally

- Read it alone, one chapter at a time
- Journal with the prompts and tools
- Share it in supervision or team reflection
- Use it as a foundation for healing groups or training sessions
- Return to it during moments of doubt, stress, or forgetting

This book does not ask for perfection. It asks for presence. And presence, when sustained, leads to remembering. And remembering is the beginning of everything.

How to Read This Book

There is no one right way to read this book. But there are two invitations:

1. Chronologically

Start at Chapter 1 and move step by step through each of the four layers. This approach allows you to follow the arc of transformation as it unfolds—from stabilizing behavior to reclaiming existential freedom.

2. Intuitively

Let your heart lead. Open to the chapter that calls you today. Whether you're navigating burnout, working with trauma, or craving reconnection with your own truth, you will find tools, stories, and reflections to meet you there.

Each chapter includes:

- A dialogue to anchor the emotional tone
- Clear science and insight for understanding
- Visuals, charts, or infographics for clarity
- Tools and practices for immediate implementation
- A Commitment Practice to make the learning stick
- End-of-chapter scientific references for those who want to go deeper

You may want to journal. You may want to reflect with your team. You may want to lead a group based on what you discover. All of that is welcome.

Just one reminder:

This book is not asking you to be better. It's inviting you to remember that you already are.

Acknowledgments

Before any words were written, there was presence. We offer deep gratitude to the people who made this book possible—not only through their time, wisdom, and support, but through the way they live.

To our clients, patients, and communities—You are our greatest teachers. Every story, every breath, every pause has shaped this book. Thank you for your courage, your trust, and your willingness to remember.

To our colleagues, clinicians, and SWEET Institute members— You are the proof that healing is possible, that systems can change, that wholeness can be practiced.

To our families, who have held space for our becoming—Thank you for your love and patience through long nights and deeper questions.

To those who came before us—The ancestors, healers, rebels, and truth-tellers—You remembered when it was dangerous. We remember now because of you.

And to every reader holding this book—Thank you for saying yes to a new way. Thank you for choosing remembering.

Part I: The Paradigm Shift

CHAPTER 1: The Fallacy of Fixing

What if no one is broken? What if we've been asking the wrong question all along?

Clinician:

I want to help them. I want to fix what's broken.

Guide:

What makes you believe they're broken?

Clinician:

Isn't that what they're here for? They're depressed, anxious, addicted, homeless, hearing voices, shutting down, acting out.

Guide:

Those are symptoms. But they're not the self.

Clinician:

So, you're saying I shouldn't treat the symptoms?

Guide:

You are to understand them. But don't confuse symptoms with identity. The moment we believe people are broken, we create a hierarchy—us and them. The Fixer and The Broken. And worse: we stop listening for who they were before the world told them who they should be.

Clinician:

But what if they do feel broken?

Guide:

Our job is to help them remember, not the event or person they believe broke them, but the truth of who they were before they ever felt broken; in order words, not the thing they believe caused their pain, but who they were before they started seeing themselves as broken.

THE PROBLEM WITH FIXING

Modern clinical systems are built around deficits, symptom checklists, pathologizing language; and treatment plans that aim to "reduce" or "eliminate" problems. But what if these are the wrong metrics? What if a person who hears voices is also the person who sings with beauty, who once laughed uncontrollably under the sun as a child?

What if the one who hoards is the one who was abandoned, and somewhere inside, still holds sacred the memory of belonging? What if we focused less on "What's wrong with you?" and more on "What interrupted your wholeness?"

SCIENCE SAYS: FIXING MISSES THE POINT

Studies in neurobiology and trauma show that behavior is adaptation, not pathology (van der Kolk, 2014). The brain responds to adversity by reshaping itself to survive (Teicher et al., 2016). The problem is, when we call the adaptation the problem, we never meet the person behind it.

Key Insight: You can't fix what isn't broken. You can only support what is forgotten.

THE FOUR LAYERS OF TRANSFORMATION

In the SWEET model, healing begins when we stop fixing and start remembering.

We do this by journeying through the four layers:

≡ THE FOUR LAYERS OF TRANSFORMATION

Layer	Focus	Goal
Conscious	Behaviors, habits, structure	Stability and empowerment
Pre-Conscious	Schemas, beliefs, patterns	Awareness and re-patterning
Unconscious	Repressed material, symbolic material	Integration and emotional liberation
Existential	Meaning, freedom, purpose	Ownership, presence, and wholeness

Every true transformation begins with the question: Where am I in this sequence?

TOOL: FROM FIXING TO REMEMBERING

Try This: The Mirror Shift Practice

1. Think of one client, patient, or person you serve whom you view as "resistant" or "difficult."
2. Instead of asking, What do I need to fix?, ask:
   a. What might they have forgotten about who they are?
   b. What might I have forgotten about who I am in this encounter?

3. Reflect:

    a. What changes in how I see them?

    b. What changes in how I show up?

Repeat daily for one week. Journal the results.

EXPERIENTIAL INSIGHT

Fixing is the path of fear. It says: "I need to control this."

Remembering is the path of love. It says: "You already are. Let me walk with you as you return to yourself."

COMMITMENT PRACTICE

Today, I choose to pause before I fix. I choose to see beneath the surface. I choose to ask:

> Who is this person—beneath the labels, beneath the wounds? Who were they before the interruption? And who am I being in their presence?

END-OF-CHAPTER SCIENTIFIC REFERENCES

- van der Kolk, B. A. (2014). The Body Keeps the Score: Brain, Mind, and Body in the Healing of Trauma. Viking.

- Teicher, M. H., Samson, J. A., Anderson, C. M., & Ohashi, K. (2016). The effects of childhood maltreatment on brain structure, function and connectivity. Nature Reviews Neuroscience, 17(10), 652–666.

- Siegel, D. J. (2012). The Developing Mind: How Relationships and the Brain Interact to Shape Who We Are. Guilford Press.

CHAPTER 2: The Pre-Conditioned Self

Before trauma, Before labels, Before roles, There was you: Whole, Curious, Alive.

Clinician:

So, if we're not here to fix people, then who are we helping them become?

Guide:

Not become; rather, Return to.

Clinician:

Return to what?

Guide:

To who they were before the conditioning. Before they were told, "Be quiet," "Don't cry," "Be strong," "Fit in," "Don't be too much." Before they were shaped by survival. Before they forgot.

Clinician:

But how do we find that self? Most people don't even know it exists.

Guide:

And yet it's never gone. It's beneath the fear, the anger, the coping, the mask.

We've seen it in glimpses—when someone laughs without shame, plays without permission, feels safe enough to be soft. That's the pre-conditioned self: Curious, Present, Loving, Creative, Whole.

REMEMBERING WHO WE WERE

The pre-conditioned self is not a concept—it's a biological and psychological reality. Infants are not born anxious, addicted, dissociated, or ashamed. They are born wired for connection, exploration, and joy (Schore, 2001; Porges, 2011). In the absence of severe disruption, children naturally attune to others, play without agenda, and express freely. But then… the conditioning begins.

"A child is not a blank slate, but a whole being. Our task is not to rewrite them, but to protect what is already complete."
— **Karen Dubin, PhD, LCSW**

THE SCIENCE OF THE EARLY SELF

- Attachment theory shows that children build internal working models of themselves and the world by how caregivers respond to their needs (Bowlby, 1988).

- Polyvagal theory reveals that our nervous systems are shaped by cues of safety or threat in early environments (Porges, 2011).

- Right brain development in infancy is responsible for emotional regulation, identity formation, and nonverbal memory—and it develops before language (Schore, 2001).

So, when a child adapts by becoming hyper-independent, people-pleasing, aggressive, withdrawn, or perfectionistic—they are not broken. They are adjusting to a world that stopped seeing who they truly were.

The Shift from Pre-Conditioned to Conditioned Self

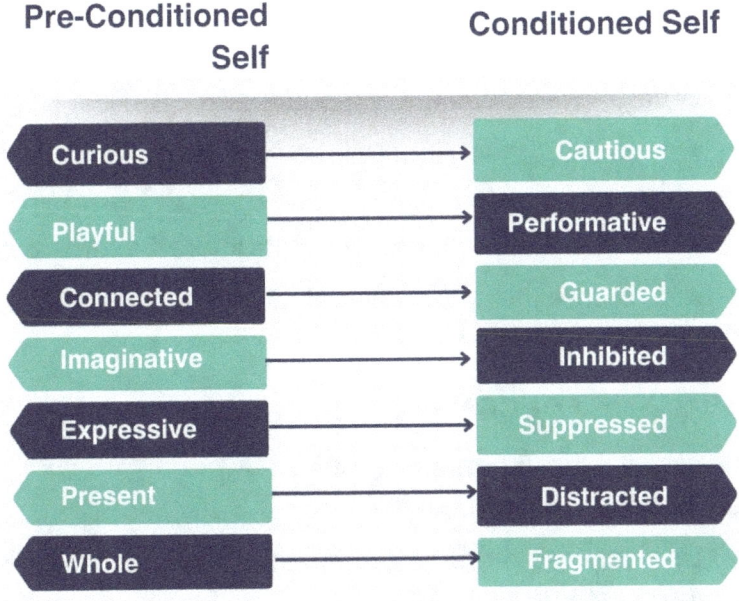

Pre-Conditioned Self → Conditioned Self

Pre-Conditioned Self	Conditioned Self
Curious	Cautious
Playful	Performative
Connected	Guarded
Imaginative	Inhibited
Expressive	Suppressed
Present	Distracted
Whole	Fragmented

TOOL: The Remembering Timeline

Instructions:

1. Draw a timeline from birth to present.

2. Mark key moments where you felt fully yourself—free, alive, unafraid.

3. Mark key moments where you began to feel shut down, masked, or shaped by others.

4. Ask: What did I learn about the world in each of those moments? What did I forget about myself?

This exercise can be done personally or as a clinical tool.

LAYER 1: THE CONSCIOUS

Behavioral practices that reawaken the pre-conditioned self:

- Daily play (yes, even adults)
- Breath awareness and embodiment
- Joy-based scheduling: "What would bring me delight today?"
- Music, dance, movement—unstructured expression

These help restore the experience of aliveness, not just the idea of it.

LAYER 2: THE PRECONSCIOUS

- Identify the inherited scripts: "Be strong." "Don't need anyone." "Stay in control."
- Use schema therapy to uncover early maladaptive patterns (Young et al., 2003).
- Begin re-authoring: Who would I be without this rule?

LAYER 3: THE UNCONSCIOUS

Dreams, slips, projections—all carry echoes of the forgotten self.

Use free association to uncover buried moments of wonder, joy, or innocence now held hostage by shame or trauma.

The unconscious remembers what the conscious mind was forced to forget.

LAYER 4: THE EXISTENTIAL

To remember is to choose.

- Choose presence over protection.
- Choose wholeness over identity.

- Choose the path of becoming again what you always were.

EXPERIENTIAL INSIGHT

The pre-conditioned self never left.

It's waiting behind the defenses we built to survive.

Remembering is not regression—it's restoration.

COMMITMENT PRACTICE

Today, I pause. I remember that once, I was whole. I was curious. I was enough. I commit to meeting others from that place, and to making space for them to remember too.

END-OF-CHAPTER SCIENTIFIC REFERENCES

- Bowlby, J. (1988). A Secure Base: Parent-Child Attachment and Healthy Human Development. Basic Books.

- Porges, S. W. (2011). The Polyvagal Theory: Neurophysiological Foundations of Emotions, Attachment, Communication, and Self-regulation. W. W. Norton & Company.

- Schore, A. N. (2001). Effects of a secure attachment relationship on right brain development, affect regulation, and infant mental health. Infant Mental Health Journal, 22(1-2), 7–66.

- Young, J. E., Klosko, J. S., & Weishaar, M. E. (2003). Schema Therapy: A Practitioner's Guide. Guilford Press.

CHAPTER 3: The Four Layers of Transformation

There is no true change without depth. And no depth without sequence.

Clinician:

Okay, I'm beginning to see it now. Remembering—not fixing. Returning—not reinventing.

But how? Where do we even begin?

Guide:

We begin at the layer we can touch. The one above the surface: behavior, breath, body, choices. Then we go deeper.

Clinician:

You're talking about layers?

Guide:

Yes. Four of them. Always in this order: Conscious. Preconscious. Unconscious. Existential. We call this the *SWEET Topographical and Existential Model of Transformation.*

Clinician:

Why does the order matter?

Guide:

Because without structure, the unconscious overwhelms. Without meaning, behavior becomes robotic. Depth without direction is chaos. Change without integration is temporary.

THE FOUR LAYERS AT A GLANCE

Layer	Focus	Goal	Methods
Conscious	Behavior, habits, lifestyle	Stability and activation	Routines, sleep, food, breathwork, CBT, coaching
Preconscious	Patterns, beliefs, schemas	Awareness and restructuring	Schema therapy, ACT, Gestalt, mindfulness
Unconscious	Repressed material, trauma, defenses	Emotional resolution and insight	Free association, dream work, psychodynamic therapy
Existential	Meaning, freedom, purpose, choice	Integration and wholeness	Existential therapy, values clarification, golden rule

WHY SEQUENCE MATTERS

You can't build meaning on top of repression.

You can't access repressed material without a stable preconscious container.

You can't rewire beliefs if behavior is chaotic.

You can't sustain change without existential choice.

Most treatment skips the middle or jumps to the bottom. That's why it doesn't last.

True transformation is layered and sequential. Integration is only possible when all four are touched.

LAYER 1: THE CONSCIOUS

This is where we start:

- Sleep hygiene
- Nutrition and hydration
- Physical activity
- Breath awareness
- Time management and structure
- Crisis planning and stabilization
- CBT tools: thought records, behavioral activation
- Daily goals, rewards, accountability

Science: Executive function improves through consistent routines (Diamond, 2013). Neuroplasticity requires repetition and novelty (Doidge, 2007).

LAYER 2: THE PRECONSCIOUS

This is the bridge between what we do and what we believe.

- Core beliefs (Young et al., 2003)
- Attachment patterns
- Internalized messages
- ACT: Defusion and values-based action
- Gestalt: Empty chair work, unfinished business
- Schema modes and inner parts

Science: Schemas are activated under stress and influence emotion, perception, and action (Beck, 2011; Young, 2003).

LAYER 3: THE UNCONSCIOUS

Here lies the hidden material:

- Early trauma
- Symbolic memories
- Dreams and nightmares
- Resistance, projection, and defense
- Repression and symbolic expression
- Techniques: free association, dream analysis, transference work

Science: Unconscious memory systems drive emotional behavior (Solms, 2002; Westen, 1999).

LAYER 4: THE EXISTENTIAL

This is where choice returns.

- Who do I choose to be?
- What meaning am I giving to my life?
- What is worth suffering for?
- What legacy am I living into?

Use existential therapy, logotherapy (Frankl, 2006), and the Golden Rule as compass:

Do unto others as you would have them do unto you.

And: Do unto yourself as you would do for the person you love most.

Existential work brings integration, peace, and purpose beyond pathology (Yalom, 1980).

THE FOUR-LAYER PYRAMID OF TRANSFORMATION

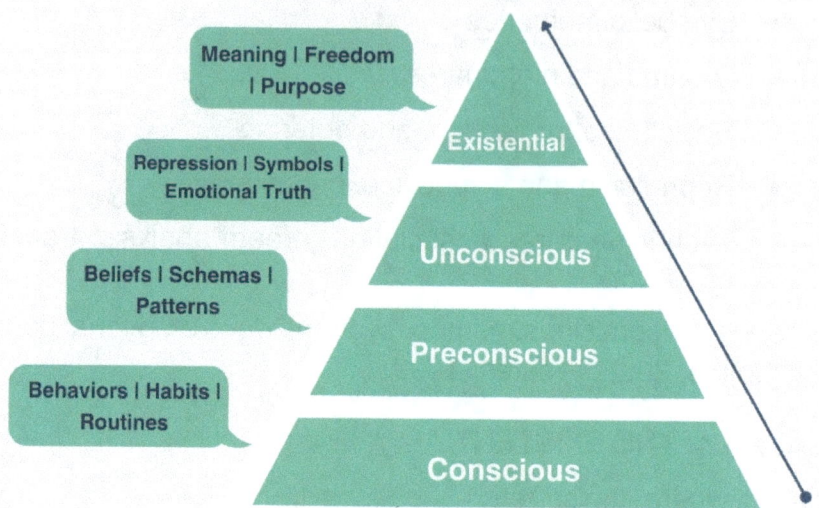

Each layer supports the next. You can't skip the foundation.

TOOL: The Layer Scan

Instructions:

Each morning or evening, pause and ask yourself:

1. Conscious: What did I do today to support my well-being?

2. Preconscious: What belief showed up today that shaped my experience?

3. Unconscious: What emotion or dream surprised me? What did I avoid?

4. Existential: What did I choose to stand for today? What meaning guided me?

Track your answers for 7 days. Watch the patterns.

EXPERIENTIAL INSIGHT

Change isn't about doing more.

It's about going deeper, one layer at a time.

Transformation is not a hack. It's a homecoming.

COMMITMENT PRACTICE

Today, I commit to honoring the sequence. I won't force insight when I need structure. I will walk the layers one by one, bearing in mind that healing is both science and remembering.

END-OF-CHAPTER SCIENTIFIC REFERENCES

- Beck, J. S. (2011). Cognitive Behavior Therapy: Basics and Beyond (2nd ed.). Guilford Press.

- Diamond, A. (2013). Executive functions. Annual Review of Psychology, 64, 135–168.

- Doidge, N. (2007). The Brain That Changes Itself: Stories of Personal Triumph from the Frontiers of Brain Science. Viking.

- Frankl, V. E. (2006). Man's Search for Meaning. Beacon Press.

- Solms, M., & Turnbull, O. (2002). The Brain and the Inner World: An Introduction to the Neuroscience of Subjective Experience. Other Press.

- Westen, D. (1999). The scientific status of unconscious processes: Is Freud really dead? Journal of the American Psychoanalytic Association, 47(4), 1061–1106.

- Yalom, I. D. (1980). Existential Psychotherapy. Basic Books.

- Young, J. E., Klosko, J. S., & Weishaar, M. E. (2003). Schema Therapy: A Practitioner's Guide. Guilford Press.

Part II: The Four Layers in Depth

CHAPTER 4: Working at the Conscious Layer

Structure first. Then depth. You can't heal what you haven't stabilized.

Clinician:

I used to think we had to start with trauma, or the inner child, or some deep insight from childhood.

Guide:

That's like trying to dig during a storm—you can't go deep when the ground keeps shifting. Depth requires calm. Depth requires safety. The conscious layer—daily habits, routines, the body—is the foundation for everything else.

Clinician:

But it seems so... basic.

Guide:

Basic is not the opposite of profound. Basic is what makes the profound possible.

If someone isn't sleeping, eating, breathing with awareness, or getting out of bed... what use is insight?

Clinician:

So conscious work is remembering too?

Guide:

It's the first act of remembering. The structure that allows the rest of the self to come online.

WHAT IS THE CONSCIOUS LAYER?

The conscious layer includes:

- Behavior
- Lifestyle choices
- Physical health
- Environmental structure
- Daily rhythms
- Cognitive awareness
- Accountability and effort

It's the most accessible layer—and the most ignored.

When clinicians skip this, we risk destabilizing clients or confusing insight with progress.

We must stabilize before we analyze.

WHY THE CONSCIOUS LAYER MATTERS

Neuroscience confirms that behavior change rewires the brain (Doidge, 2007).

- Sleep regulates emotion and cognitive function (Walker, 2017).
- Physical activity reduces depression and boosts neurogenesis (Ratey, 2008).
- Consistent routines build executive functioning (Diamond, 2013).
- Breathwork activates the parasympathetic nervous system and downregulates fear (Porges, 2011).

In other words: structure sets the stage for safety. Safety opens the door to depth.

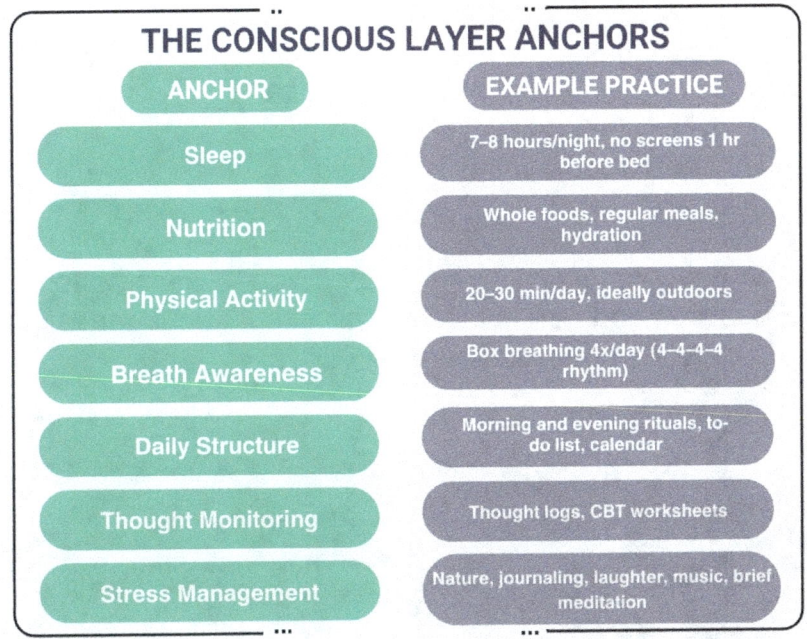

THE CONSCIOUS LAYER ANCHORS

ANCHOR	EXAMPLE PRACTICE
Sleep	7–8 hours/night, no screens 1 hr before bed
Nutrition	Whole foods, regular meals, hydration
Physical Activity	20–30 min/day, ideally outdoors
Breath Awareness	Box breathing 4x/day (4–4–4–4 rhythm)
Daily Structure	Morning and evening rituals, to-do list, calendar
Thought Monitoring	Thought logs, CBT worksheets
Stress Management	Nature, journaling, laughter, music, brief meditation

TOOL: The Conscious Layer Checklist

Instructions

Complete this checklist each morning or each night by reflecting on the past 24 hours. For each "yes," give yourself 1 point. For each "no," give 0 points. Be honest and gentle with yourself.

Complete each morning or night:

- Did I sleep 7+ hours?
- Did I move my body for at least 20 minutes?
- Did I breathe mindfully at least once?
- Did I follow a basic routine or schedule?
- Did I hydrate and eat whole food?
- Did I challenge or track a negative thought?
- Did I create space for one moment of peace?

39

Score:

0–2 = Survival mode

3–5 = Stabilizing

6–7 = Anchored

Practice Tip

Repeat daily for 7 days. Use your scores to track patterns in your habits, mood, and mindset. This is not about perfection — it's about self-awareness and progress.

LAYERED INTEGRATION: WHERE IT FITS

Layer	Action
Conscious	Anchor habits and routines
Preconscious	Become aware of beliefs influencing behavior
Unconscious	Watch for what the body resists or avoids
Existential	Reclaim choice and responsibility in daily life

Conscious practices are the soil for deeper roots.

COMMON MISTAKES AT THIS LAYER

- **Over-spiritualizing**: Using meditation to avoid behavior change
- **Insight overload**: Endless journaling with no routine or movement
- **Avoiding discipline**: Mistaking freedom for lack of structure

- **Hyper-focus on others**: Ignoring sleep and food while rescuing everyone else

These patterns reinforce the conditioned self. The conscious layer interrupts them.

CLINICAL APPLICATION

In sessions, begin with this question: What did your morning look like today?

If your patient is dysregulated, start here:

- Walk and talk instead of sit and analyze
- Explore bedtime routines before childhood trauma
- Track mood alongside hydration and movement

Remember: Without a stabilized body, the mind rebels.

Without a rhythm, healing gets lost in the noise.

EXPERIENTIAL INSIGHT

Daily structure is not a cage—it's a key.

It is how we begin to say:

I matter.

I am capable of showing up.

I choose to return to myself.

COMMITMENT PRACTICE

Today, I commit to anchoring the basics. I will not shame the body that has protected me. I will nourish it. I will rest it. I will breathe with it. I will remember that healing begins here—where I can reach. Where I can act. Where I choose to begin.

END-OF-CHAPTER SCIENTIFIC REFERENCES

- Doidge, N. (2007). The Brain That Changes Itself. Viking.

- Diamond, A. (2013). Executive functions. Annual Review of Psychology, 64, 135–168.

- Porges, S. W. (2011). The Polyvagal Theory. Norton.

- Ratey, J. J. (2008). Spark: The Revolutionary New Science of Exercise and the Brain. Little, Brown Spark.

- Walker, M. (2017). Why We Sleep: Unlocking the Power of Sleep and Dreams. Scribner.

CHAPTER 5: Entering the Preconscious

This is the space between what we do and why we do it.

Clinician:

They say they want to change. They start strong. Then they stop.

They know better—but it's like something else takes over.

Guide:

Something does. But it's not random. It's patterned.

The preconscious is where those patterns live. It's the space just beneath awareness. You don't always see it—but it shapes everything.

Clinician:

So, they're not being resistant?

Guide:

They're being loyal. Loyal to old beliefs, old stories, old survival strategies.

The preconscious is not the enemy—it's the script they've been following for decades.

We don't need to fight it. We need to reveal it.

WHAT IS THE PRECONSCIOUS LAYER?

The preconscious is the level just beneath conscious awareness.

It includes:

- Core beliefs
- Early adaptive schemas
- Internalized messages
- Unfinished emotional business
- Attachment patterns
- Default self-talk and reactions

It is not fully unconscious, but it is often automatic and unexamined.

This is the domain of the Conditioned Self.

"Until you make the unconscious conscious, it will direct your life and you will call it fate." — Carl Jung

SCIENTIFIC INSIGHT: THE POWER OF SCHEMAS

Schemas are deeply rooted mental frameworks shaped by early experiences.

They filter how we see the world, ourselves, and others (Young et al., 2003).

Common maladaptive schemas include:

- **Abandonment**: "People always leave."
- **Defectiveness**: "I'm not good enough."
- **Mistrust**: "People will hurt me."
- **Failure**: "I'll never succeed."
- **Emotional Deprivation**: "No one will meet my needs."

These beliefs were once protective. But they now fuel self-sabotage, burnout, and relationship pain.

SURFACE VS. SCHEMA

Behavior	Underlying Schema
Avoids Relationships	Mistrust / Abandonment
Overworks and Burns Out	Defectiveness / Failure
People Pleases	Subjugation / Unrelenting Standards
Gives Up Easily	Inadequacy / Pessimism
Constantly Seeks Approval	Recognition-Seeking / Shame

LAYERED INTEGRATION

Layer	Focus At This Stage
Conscious	Observe behavior, track triggers
Preconscious	Identify schemas, emotional patterns, internalized rules
Unconscious	Discover emotional origins, memories, repressed content
Existential	Choose new guiding values beyond the schema

TOOL: Schema Mapping Exercise

Step 1: Identify the Pattern

What area of life do you struggle with most (work, relationships, self-worth)?

Step 2: Explore the Thought

What belief shows up when things go wrong?

Step 3: Feel the Emotion

What do you feel when that belief activates?

Step 4: Trace the Origin

When did you first feel this way? What story did you create to survive?

Step 5: Name the Schema

Choose from common schemas or name your own.

Step 6: Rewrite the Message

What would your pre-conditioned self say instead?

INTERVENTIONS FOR THE PRECONSCIOUS

- **Schema Therapy:** Identify, name, and re-script maladaptive beliefs
- **ACT (Acceptance & Commitment Therapy):** Defusion from thoughts + values-based living
- **Mindfulness:** Notice patterns without judgment
- **Gestalt:** Dialogue with parts (inner child, inner critic)
- **Imagery Rescripting:** Create new emotional outcomes for old situations

These interventions make the invisible, visible—and give clients choice.

CLINICAL INSIGHT

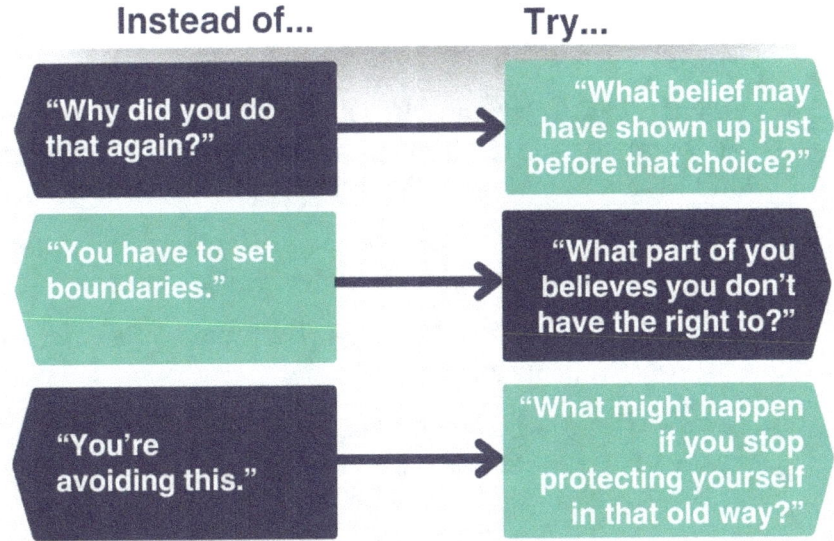

Instead of...	Try...
"Why did you do that again?"	"What belief may have shown up just before that choice?"
"You have to set boundaries."	"What part of you believes you don't have the right to?"
"You're avoiding this."	"What might happen if you stop protecting yourself in that old way?"

EXPERIENTIAL INSIGHT

The preconscious is a mirror.

Every repeated conflict is an invitation to see what you've been believing.

Every reaction is a messenger.

It says: You don't have to be this version anymore.

COMMITMENT PRACTICE

Today, I commit to pausing between reaction and response. I will ask: What belief just showed up? Is it true? Is it mine? Is it current? I choose to question the script I inherited—and to write a new one.

END-OF-CHAPTER SCIENTIFIC REFERENCES

- Young, J. E., Klosko, J. S., & Weishaar, M. E. (2003). Schema Therapy: A Practitioner's Guide. Guilford Press.

- Hayes, S. C., Strosahl, K. D., & Wilson, K. G. (2011). Acceptance and Commitment Therapy: The Process and Practice of Mindful Change. Guilford Press.

- Linehan, M. M. (1993). Cognitive-Behavioral Treatment of Borderline Personality Disorder. Guilford Press.

- Beck, A. T. (2011). Cognitive Therapy of Personality Disorders. Guilford Press.

- Neff, K. D. (2003). The development and validation of a scale to measure self-compassion. Self and Identity, 2(3), 223–250.

CHAPTER 6: Meeting the Unconscious

The part of you you've never met is the one still running the show.

Clinician:

Okay, I've worked with their behaviors. I've helped them identify beliefs. But then they sabotage. They ghost the process. They get flooded with emotion out of nowhere.

Guide:

That's the unconscious. It doesn't knock—it erupts.

Clinician:

So, what do I do? It feels like I'm losing them.

Guide:

You're not. You're being invited into a deeper room. The unconscious isn't trying to hurt you or your client. It's trying to speak. But you have to know its language.

Clinician:

Which is?

Guide:

Symbol. Resistance. Projection. Repetition. Dreams. Slips. Emotion out of context.

What was repressed is never gone—it's just buried.

To remember, we must be willing to go down there.

WHAT IS THE UNCONSCIOUS LAYER?

The unconscious holds:

- Repressed memories and emotions
- Unresolved trauma
- Early developmental pain
- Internal conflicts
- Dissociated parts
- Symbolic material: dreams, fantasies, metaphors

These are often too painful, threatening, or overwhelming to face at the time they were formed—so the mind buried them.

But buried doesn't mean inactive.

"The past is never dead. It's not even past." — William Faulkner

FREUD WAS RIGHT (AND SO WAS NEUROSCIENCE)

Freud described the unconscious as the seat of repressed desire, defense, and conflict.

Modern neuroscience shows that:

- Implicit memory holds emotional experiences we can't recall but still react to (Siegel, 2012).
- The amygdala stores fear-based learning without conscious access (LeDoux, 1996).
- Early trauma shapes procedural memory and bodily responses (van der Kolk, 2014).
- Dreams are not random—they're symbolic reorganizations of unresolved affect (Solms, 2000).

COMMON UNCONSCIOUS EXPRESSIONS IN CLINICAL WORK

Manifestation	Unconscious Process
Sudden anger at therapist	Transference / Projection
Dream of drowning	Overwhelm, loss of emotional boundaries
Repeating same relationship	Repetition compulsion
Forgetting session time	Resistance / avoidance of insight
Chronic fatigue in sessions	Dissociation / emotional shutdown
Panic with no trigger	Implicit trauma memory activation

Don't interpret too quickly. Approach with curiosity, not control.

TOOL: The Symbol Tracker

Use this in session or in journaling.

When an emotional or symbolic moment arises:

1. What just happened (the trigger)?
2. What emotion showed up (and at what intensity)?
3. What image, memory, or body sensation accompanied it?
4. What might this symbolize? (Even if it seems silly.)
5. When in life have you felt something similar?

This brings the unconscious to the threshold of preconscious awareness—where healing becomes possible.

INTERVENTIONS FOR THE UNCONSCIOUS

- **Free Association:** Speak without censoring. Follow the emotional current.

- **Dream Analysis:** Record dreams daily. Identify symbols, themes, and emotional tone.

- **Active Imagination:** Engage inner figures in dialogue (Jungian).

- **Somatic Tracking:** Where in the body does the emotion live? What's its shape, color, or story?

- **Projective Techniques:** Art, poetry, metaphor, role-play

- **Working Through:** Revisit, relive, resolve—until reaction becomes reflection

LAYERED INTEGRATION	
Layer	**In the Context of the Unconscious**
Conscious	Notice avoidance, denial, rationalization
Preconscious	Identify surface beliefs masking deeper wounds
Unconscious	Explore emotional origins, symbols, and unresolved pain
Existential	Accept, integrate, and choose new meaning

You can't shift what you don't face. But you don't have to face it all at once.

EXPERIENTIAL INSIGHT

The unconscious is not your enemy.

It is the part of you that carried the unbearable until you could return for it.

To remember fully is to re-own what was disowned.

COMMITMENT PRACTICE

Today, I will not rush past discomfort. I will ask what part of me is speaking. I will make space for the forgotten, the shamed, the silenced. I am not afraid of the dark—not when I remember that every truth, once held with love, becomes light.

END-OF-CHAPTER SCIENTIFIC REFERENCES

- Freud, S. (1915). The Unconscious.

- Siegel, D. J. (2012). The Developing Mind. Guilford Press.

- Solms, M. (2000). Dreaming and REM sleep are controlled by different brain mechanisms. Behavioral and Brain Sciences, 23(6), 843–850.

- van der Kolk, B. A. (2014). The Body Keeps the Score. Viking.

- LeDoux, J. (1996). The Emotional Brain: The Mysterious Underpinnings of Emotional Life. Simon & Schuster.

- Westen, D. (1999). The scientific status of unconscious processes. JAPA, 47(4), 1061–1106.

CHAPTER 7: The Existential Integration

At the end of all healing is choice. At the heart of all change is freedom.

Clinician:

They've changed their behaviors.

They've uncovered their beliefs.

They've touched deep pain.

Now they are asking, "What's next?"

Guide:

Now comes the most radical act of all: choosing.

Not because of pressure. Not because of pain.

But because they finally can.

Clinician:

Choose what?

Guide:

Who to be.

What to value.

How to live.

Why to live.

Clinician:

That's terrifying.

Guide:

That's freedom.

And it's what they were always moving toward—beneath the pain, beneath the protection, beneath the pattern.

They were searching for meaning.

Your job isn't to give it to them. Your job is to create the space for them to remember it.

WHAT IS THE EXISTENTIAL LAYER?

The existential layer is the realm of:

- Meaning
- Responsibility
- Purpose
- Freedom
- Ethics
- Presence
- Death, legacy, and transcendence

This layer cannot be imposed. It must be chosen. It is the domain of agency.

"Between stimulus and response, there is a space. In that space is our power to choose our response. In our response lies our growth and our freedom."

— Viktor Frankl

WHY THE EXISTENTIAL LAYER MATTERS

After healing, there must be integration.

Otherwise, we remain trapped in the cycle of "more healing," "more therapy," "more introspection."

But healing is not the goal.

Living is.

Existential work asks:

What is your life now for?

What legacy are you creating?

What do you stand for, when the pain is no longer in charge?

KEY THEMES OF EXISTENTIAL WORK	
Theme	**Questions to Explore**
Freedom	What is in your control? What will you do with it?
Responsibility	What do you need to take ownership of? Where have you been waiting for permission?
Meaning	What gives you a reason to keep going—even on the hardest days?
Choice	What do you choose to believe, today? What do you choose to embody, today?
Mortality	If your life ended tomorrow, what would remain unfinished, unsaid, unlived?
Presence	What are you avoiding now? What would happen if you turned toward it?

THE GOLDEN RULE AS EXISTENTIAL COMPASS

The simplest, most powerful tool at this layer:

Do unto others as you would have them do unto you.

And do unto yourself as you would do for the person you love most.

This re-centers morality, wholeness, and human connection in everyday action.

In a fragmented world, the Golden Rule restores belonging and integrity.

TOOL: Existential Alignment Map

1. What matters most to me right now?
2. What daily actions reflect that? What contradicts it?
3. What legacy am I building—by accident or by design?
4. What does my suffering invite me to serve?
5. What values do I want to embody in this season of life?
6. What decision do I need to make today, to align with my purpose?

Review weekly. Let your answers evolve.

CLINICAL PRACTICE INSIGHT

Use existential questioning not as analysis, but as an invitation to ownership.

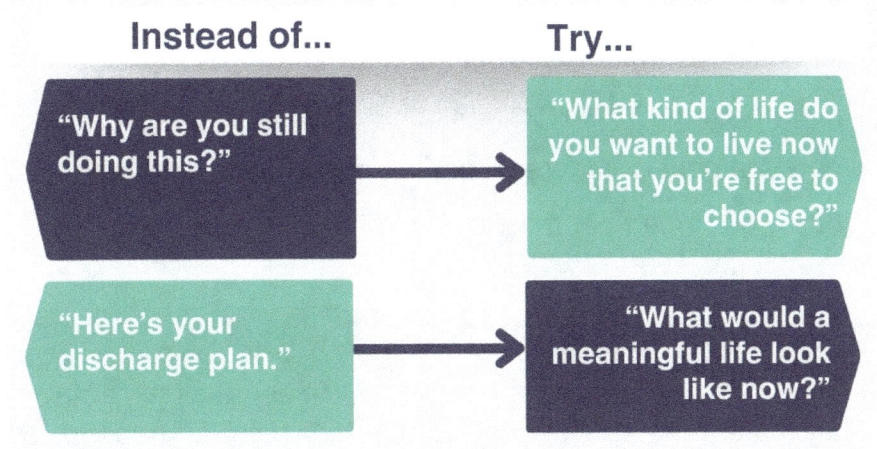

This is the transition from treatment to transformation.

LAYERED INTEGRATION

Layer	Existential Integration
Conscious	What routines align with your chosen purpose?
Preconscious	What beliefs must evolve to support the life you now choose?
Unconscious	What pain, now integrated, becomes fuel for your mission?
Existential	Who are you becoming—on purpose, by choice, with meaning?

You are not what happened to you. You are what you do with it now.

EXPERIENTIAL INSIGHT

The existential layer is the still point.

The quiet center where pain becomes purpose.

Where the past is honored—but no longer holds the pen.

Where you remember that life is not something to survive—it is something to live.

COMMITMENT PRACTICE

Today, I choose to live on purpose. I will act in alignment with what matters most. I will not be ruled by pain, by habit, or by fear. I am free. I am responsible. I am here.

END-OF-CHAPTER SCIENTIFIC REFERENCES

- Frankl, V. E. (2006). Man's Search for Meaning. Beacon Press.

- Yalom, I. D. (1980). Existential Psychotherapy. Basic Books.

- van Deurzen, E. (2002). Existential Counselling and Psychotherapy in Practice. Sage.

- Bugental, J. F. T. (1987). The Art of the Psychotherapist. Norton.

- Wong, P. T. P. (2012). The human quest for meaning: Theories, research, and applications. Routledge.

Part III: Integration and Application

CHAPTER 8: The Practice of Remembering

Not healing. Not fixing. Not finding. Remembering.

Clinician:

It's all starting to make sense now. We've built the routines. We've named the patterns. We've faced the buried pain. And we've reclaimed choice.

Guide:

Now comes the simplest and most profound practice of all.

Remembering.

Clinician:

But remembering what?

Guide:

Who you were before the world interrupted, Before the shame, Before the silence, Before the schema, the sabotage, the diagnosis, the name tag. You came into this world whole. You never stopped being whole. But you forgot. And now, you remember.

WHAT IS REMEMBERING?

Remembering is not recalling facts or events.

It is the process of reconnecting with the pre-conditioned self:

- Curious
- Alive
- Joyful
- Embodied
- Imaginative
- Compassionate
- Free

Remembering is spiritual, psychological, and biological reconnection.

It is the undoing of forgetting.

SCIENCE OF REMEMBERING

- Neuroplasticity confirms that repeated experiences rewire brain identity maps (Doidge, 2007).
- Attachment repair creates new implicit memory that reshapes self-concept (Siegel, 2012).
- Compassion-focused therapy activates the parasympathetic nervous system and reduces self-criticism (Gilbert, 2009).
- Inner child work bridges developmental gaps, restoring spontaneity and emotional access (Schore, 2003).

Remembering isn't fantasy—it's restorative neurobiology.

REMEMBERING PRACTICES

1. Daily Inner Child Check-In

- Ask: "What would 5-year-old me want to do today?"
- Draw, dance, nap, explore—whatever evokes joy.

2. Self-Affirming Rituals

- Choose one statement from the pre-conditioned self and repeat it daily:
    - "I am enough."
    - "I was born whole."
    - "Joy is my birthright."
    - "I am not who hurt me."
    - "I am not my trauma."

3. Joy-Based Scheduling

- Schedule at least 15 minutes each day to do something with no outcome agenda—just experience the joy.

4. Embodied Presence

- Walk barefoot. Dance freely. Sing in the shower. Breathe deeply.
- Re-inhabit your body as your home.

5. Mirror Work

- Look yourself in the eye.
- Say: "I remember you. You never left. I see you."

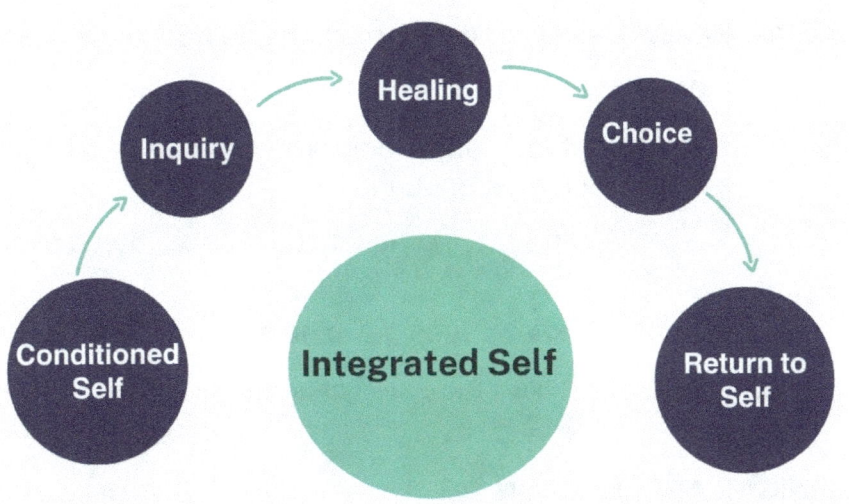

The Arc of Remembering

Remembering is not going back.

It is going forward with all of you intact.

LAYERED INTEGRATION THROUGH REMEMBERING

Layer	Remembering Practice
Conscious	Daily rituals, structure, and embodiment
Preconscious	Inner re-parenting and belief reauthoring
Unconscious	Symbol work, dreams, integration of disowned parts
Existential	Choosing to live, love, and lead from wholeness

TOOL: Remembering Journal Prompts

Use these daily, weekly, or during moments of doubt:

- What part of myself have I forgotten today?
- What did I love doing before I was told it was silly, too much, or not enough?
- What would I do if I knew I could never be unloved again?
- What do I know, deep down, to be true about me?
- What joy have I denied myself that I can return to— just for today?

CLINICAL APPLICATION

Use remembering in therapy with:

- Clients in identity foreclosure
- Clients post-crisis or post-discharge
- Long-term trauma survivors ready for meaning re-construction
- Creative or spiritual reawakening

Remember: this is not regression. It is restoration.

When your client smiles with wonder, laughs without apology, or cries because they feel seen—that's remembering.

EXPERIENTIAL INSIGHT

You were never meant to be fixed.

You were meant to be free.

This work—the conscious, the preconscious, the unconscious, the existential—was never about changing who you are.

It was about removing everything that made you forget.

Now, you remember.

And because you do, you help others remember too.

COMMITMENT PRACTICE

Today, I will not seek to be more. I will return to what I already am. I remember joy. I remember softness. I remember breath, curiosity, and wonder. I remember me.

END-OF-CHAPTER SCIENTIFIC REFERENCES

- Doidge, N. (2007). The Brain That Changes Itself. Viking.

- Gilbert, P. (2009). The Compassionate Mind. Constable & Robinson.

- Siegel, D. J. (2012). The Developing Mind. Guilford Press.

- Schore, A. N. (2003). Affect Dysregulation and Disorders of the Self. Norton.

- Neff, K. (2011). Self-Compassion: The Proven Power of Being Kind to Yourself. William Morrow.

CHAPTER 9: Remembering in Clinical Practice

You are not here to fix. You are here to hold the mirror.

Clinician:

I want to do this differently now. Not fix. Not push. Not manage.

Guide:

Then remember who you are too.

Clinician:

What do you mean?

Guide:

You can't guide someone back to themselves if you've forgotten your own wholeness.

The clinician who remembers brings presence, not performance. Curiosity, not control.

And that changes everything.

Clinician:

So clinical work becomes sacred work?

Guide:

It always was. We just forgot.

WHAT REMEMBERING LOOKS LIKE IN PRACTICE

In clinical sessions, remembering isn't a technique—it's a stance, a lens, a presence.

It means:

- We're not trying to diagnose wholeness—we're trying to recognize it.

- We don't rush to teach—we listen for what's already known.

- We slow down. We ask different questions. We model what it means to feel safe being.

THE REMEMBERING CLINICIAN: A NEW PARADIGM

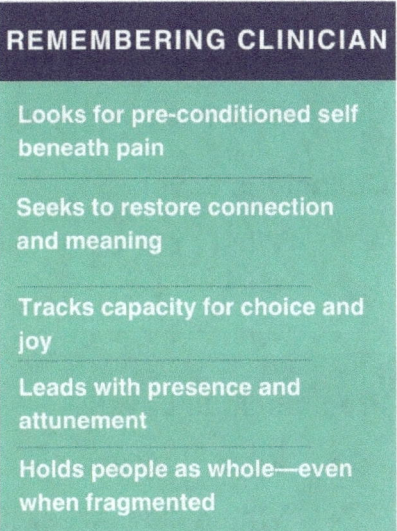

TRADITIONAL CLINICIAN	REMEMBERING CLINICIAN
Focuses on pathology	Looks for pre-conditioned self beneath pain
Seeks to reduce symptoms	Seeks to restore connection and meaning
Tracks compliance	Tracks capacity for choice and joy
Leads with problem-solving	Leads with presence and attunement
Treats people as cases	Holds people as whole—even when fragmented

"The remembering clinician does not look for deficits. They look for sparks."

— **Karen Dubin, PhD, LCSW**

SCIENTIFIC FOUNDATIONS OF REMEMBERING PRACTICE

- Therapeutic presence improves outcomes across modalities (Geller & Greenberg, 2012).

- Attachment-informed care supports re-regulation through attuned responsiveness (Schore, 2001).

- Post-traumatic growth requires the clinician to believe in a future beyond trauma (Tedeschi & Calhoun, 2004).

- Neuroception of safety (Porges, 2011) is influenced by clinician voice tone, posture, and facial expression.

The science is clear: The way you are with someone changes their brain.

REMEMBERING QUESTIONS IN SESSION

Use these across the layers:

Conscious Layer

- "What's one small thing you did today that honored your well-being?"

- "What brings you energy, even a little?"

Preconscious Layer

- "What story about yourself showed up this week?"

- "Where did that belief come from? Do you still want it?"

Unconscious Layer

- "What emotion surprised you?"

- "What did your dream or nightmare feel like?"

Existential Layer

- "What kind of life do you want now?"
- "If pain isn't your compass, what will be?"

TOOL: Remembering-Based Treatment Planning

Replace "symptom goals" with:

REMEMBERING-BASED TREATMENT PLANNING	
Old Format	**Remembering-Based Format**
Reduce depressive symptoms	Reconnect with sources of joy, energy, and identity
Improve medication compliance	Strengthen sense of choice, ownership, and self-advocacy
Decrease substance use	Restore contact with core needs and inner wholeness
Increase engagement in services	Cultivate trust, safety, and purpose in the therapeutic space

You can still use SMART goals—but center them in self, not symptoms.

REMEMBERING AS SUPERVISION AND ORGANIZA-TIONAL PRACTICE

Leaders and supervisors:

Ask your team—not just "What's the treatment plan?" but:

- "What part of the resident's pre-conditioned self have you glimpsed?"
- "How are you modeling presence?"
- "What part of you is invited to heal in this work?"

Remembering is not just for clients. It's for clinicians, teams, and systems.

EXPERIENTIAL INSIGHT

You are not a technician. You are a mirror.

And when you model safety, softness, spaciousness, and presence,

you help people remember who they were before the world told them otherwise.

COMMITMENT PRACTICE

Today, I will remember that I am not here to fix. I am here to accompany. I will slow down. I will see the spark. I will ask better questions. I will hold the mirror steady, with reverence and humility. Because the person before me is already whole. My job is to help them remember.

END-OF-CHAPTER SCIENTIFIC REFERENCES

- Geller, S. M., & Greenberg, L. S. (2012). Therapeutic Presence: A Mindful Approach to Effective Therapy. APA.

- Porges, S. W. (2011). The Polyvagal Theory. Norton.

- Schore, A. N. (2001). Effects of a secure attachment on right brain development. Infant Mental Health Journal, 22(1-2), 7–66.

- Tedeschi, R. G., & Calhoun, L. G. (2004). Posttraumatic growth: Conceptual foundations and empirical evidence. Psychological Inquiry, 15(1), 1–18.

- Siegel, D. J. (2010). The Mindful Therapist. Norton.

CHAPTER 10: Systems That Forget

What if the problem isn't just individual forgetting? What if the systems forgot first?

Clinician:

I can see it now. People aren't broken—they're buried. But the system… it still treats them like they're broken.

Guide:

Because the system has forgotten too.

Clinician:

Forgotten what?

Guide:

That it was never meant to fix people. It was meant to serve them. But somewhere along the way, systems started to believe the same lies trauma taught people: That people are problems, that control equals safety, that performance is more important than presence.

Clinician:

So, the forgetting didn't start with the person?

Guide:

It started long before. And healing is to happen on both sides.

WHEN SYSTEMS FORGET

We've built institutions—schools, hospitals, shelters, clinics—not around remembering, but around compliance, performance, and pathology.

Here's how systems forget:

System Behavior	Underlying Message
Rigid rules over human needs	"You don't matter—only order does."
One-size-fits-all treatment plans	"You are a diagnosis, not a person."
Discharge as a measure of success	"Once you're functioning, you're no longer our concern."
Focus on paperwork over connection	"Productivity matters more than presence."
Lack of trauma-informed supervision	"Your pain is irrelevant to your role."

Systemic forgetting is institutionalized dissociation.

THE COST OF SYSTEMIC FORGETTING

- **Burnout among clinicians:** Disconnection from purpose and values (Maslach & Leiter, 2016)

- **Re-traumatization of clients:** Dehumanizing environments echo early wounds (SAMHSA, 2014)

- **High turnover and moral injury:** Helpers can no longer align with the mission

- **Ineffective outcomes:** Symptom suppression without self-reclamation

REMEMBERING SYSTEMS LOOK DIFFERENT

REMEMBERING SYSTEMS LOOK DIFFERENT

FORGETTING SYSTEM	REMEMBERING SYSTEM
Prioritizes control	Prioritizes safety and trust
Seeks efficiency at the cost of humanity	Designs processes around human dignity
Disempowers clients	Co-creates meaning and direction
Measures success in discharge	Measures success in connection, growth, and purpose
Silences staff pain	Builds reflection and healing into the culture

TOOL: The System Mirror Checklist

Use in team meetings, organizational reviews, or supervision:

1. How do our policies reflect human dignity? Where do they violate it?

2. Do we make room for staff to process, reflect, and grow—or just to produce?

3. Are we building cultures of fear or of safety?

4. Do we assume people are broken—or do we trust in their wholeness?

5. Is remembering a part of our mission—or are we just managing symptoms?

SCIENTIFIC FOUNDATIONS FOR SYSTEM CHANGE

- Trauma-Informed Care shifts systems from "What's wrong with you?" to "What happened to you?" (SAMHSA, 2014)
- Organizational compassion reduces burnout and increases client engagement (West et al., 2011)
- Participatory design improves outcomes by involving clients in shaping their care (Bate & Robert, 2007)
- Reflective supervision enhances provider resilience and therapeutic effectiveness (Emde & Wise, 2003)

FROM POLICY TO PRACTICE: QUESTIONS TO ASK

- Is remembering embedded in onboarding, supervision, and performance evaluation?
- Do we offer choice, collaboration, and voice to those we serve?
- Are staff taught to recognize their own conditioned responses—not just those of their clients?
- Do we allow time for slowness, story, and stillness in our workflows?

REMEMBERING IS CONTAGIOUS

When systems remember...

- Staff soften.
- Clients breathe.
- Leaders lead with humanity.
- Outcomes improve, not because we control better— but because we connect deeper.

EXPERIENTIAL INSIGHT

You don't have to change the whole system at once.

But you can be the one who remembers.

In your session. In your notes. In your meetings. In your tone.

And from you, the remembering spreads.

COMMITMENT PRACTICE

Today, I commit to disrupting forgetting. I will not confuse policies with people. I will not trade presence for performance. I will ask better questions, listen longer, and build safer spaces—where remembering can take root, not just in individuals, but in the institutions meant to serve them.

END-OF-CHAPTER SCIENTIFIC REFERENCES

- Maslach, C., & Leiter, M. P. (2016). Burnout: A Multidimensional Perspective. CRC Press.

- SAMHSA. (2014). Trauma-Informed Care in Behavioral Health Services (Treatment Improvement Protocol Series 57).

- West, M. A., et al. (2011). Caring for people who care: The impact of compassionate leadership. The King's Fund.

- Bate, P., & Robert, G. (2007). Bringing User Experience to Healthcare Improvement. Radcliffe Publishing.

- Emde, R. N., & Wise, B. K. (2003). Reflective supervision and its impact on early childhood intervention. Zero to Three, 24(2), 9–14.

CHAPTER 11: Stories of Remembering

This is how it looks. This is how it sounds. This is how it feels when someone remembers.

Vignette 1: She Sang Again

She had not sung in 18 years.

Not since the night her uncle came into her room and left her silent.

Not since the school counselor told her to write about it instead.

Not since the church told her to forgive and forget.

In session, she hummed under her breath—so soft we almost missed it.

A note. Then another. A tremble. Then strength.

We paused the agenda.

We breathed with her.

She cried—not because she was sad.

But because the sound coming from her nose felt like a resurrection.

She sang again.

And in that moment, she remembered.

Vignette 2: The Man With the Closed Fist

Every session, his fists were clenched.

He'd sit rigid in the corner, counting exits, scanning my eyes.

"I don't talk," he'd say.

So, we didn't talk.

We walked the hallways in silence.

Tossed a ball. Watered a plant. Shared a sandwich.

Week six. I asked if he knew his fists were always tight.

He didn't.

He looked at his hands like they belonged to someone else.

"What would happen if you opened them?" I asked.

"I don't know," he whispered. "Maybe something would fall out."

That day, they opened. Just a little.

Inside wasn't violence.

Inside was fear. And love.

And a boy who hadn't been held in years.

He remembered.

Vignette 3: The Mirror

She used to avoid mirrors.

They lied, she said.

They showed her what the world taught her to see:

Too dark. Too loud. Too much.

One day, we sat in front of a mirror together.

"What do you see?" I asked.

She looked. Then turned away.

We waited.

She looked again.

"I see someone who survived," she said.

Then, after a pause:

"I see someone who was never the problem."

Vignette 4: Joy Returned Without Permission

He had been clean for 14 months, but joy still felt dangerous.

He said it reminded him of the high.

Too much light felt like temptation.

We honored that.

Until the day he laughed at a joke he told himself.

He laughed like it surprised him.

He laughed like it betrayed something.

Then he looked at me and said:

"Maybe I don't have to pay for joy anymore."

Vignette 5: The Clinician's Remembering

She had been doing this work for 22 years.

Burned out. Kind. Smart. Tired.

She came to supervision and said, "I don't know if I'm helping anymore."

We asked her: "When did you last feel alive in a session?"

She paused. Smiled.

"There was this moment. A client closed her eyes and said, 'I feel safe.' I didn't say anything. I just breathed with her."

We reminded her: That moment was the work.

She exhaled. Her shoulders softened.

"I forgot," she said.

Then, "Thank you. I remember now."

TOOL: Reflective Story Prompt for Clinicians

Use this as a personal journaling or team supervision tool:

- Describe a moment when a client remembered something about who they are.
- What did it look like?
- What did it sound like?
- What did it feel like in the room?
- How did you show up differently in that moment?
- What did you remember?

EXPERIENTIAL INSIGHT

The most profound healing moments are rarely loud.

They are felt in breath, in pause, in tears that don't need words.

They are the sacred unfolding of a self that was always there.

COMMITMENT PRACTICE

Today, I will slow down enough to witness remembering. I will not measure transformation by volume. I will honor the smallest shifts. The softest openings. The most honest sighs. I will celebrate every breath that returns home.

CHAPTER 12: The Revolution of Wholeness

Healing is not a trend. It is a revolution. And it begins with re-membering.

Clinician:

So, this is the end?

Guide:

No. This is the beginning. You've remembered. Now, help others do the same.

Clinician:

But I'm just one person.

Guide:

Every revolution starts with one remembering. And then another. And then another. We don't need louder voices. We need more clear ones.

More calm ones.

More whole ones.

WHAT IF REMEMBERING BECAME THE NORM?

What if instead of being systems of symptom suppression, our institutions were places of identity restoration? What if schools helped children preserve their wholeness? What if clinicians were trained in curiosity instead of control? What if our policies were written by those who had remembered themselves? What if people weren't discharged after stabilization—but guided home to themselves? This is not a utopia. This is a possibility.

THE NEW STANDARD OF CARE

Let's imagine a new model of healing—across every profession and system:

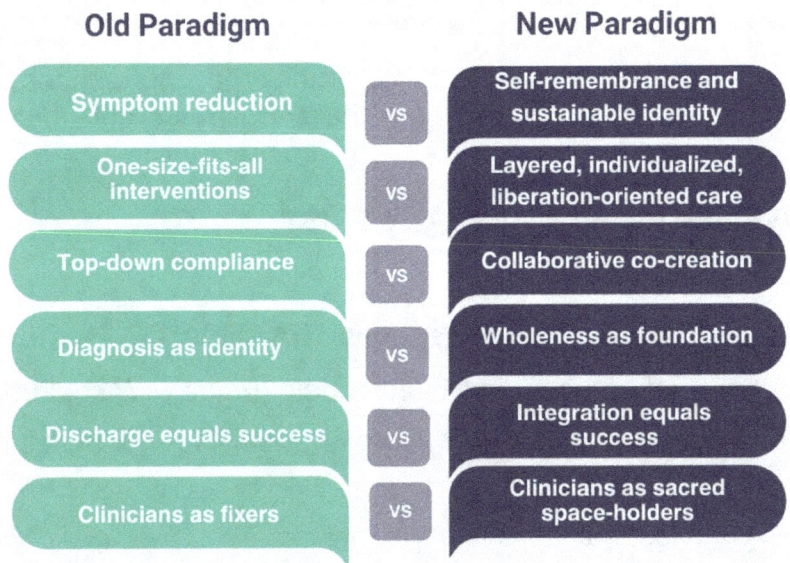

Old Paradigm		New Paradigm
Symptom reduction	vs	Self-remembrance and sustainable identity
One-size-fits-all interventions	vs	Layered, individualized, liberation-oriented care
Top-down compliance	vs	Collaborative co-creation
Diagnosis as identity	vs	Wholeness as foundation
Discharge equals success	vs	Integration equals success
Clinicians as fixers	vs	Clinicians as sacred space-holders

The remembering model is not a technique—it's a return.

TOOLS FOR SPREADING THE REVOLUTION

1. Start Where You Are

- Integrate the 4 Layers into your work today: behavior, belief, buried pain, and meaning.

- Anchor presence into your role, whether clinician, teacher, leader, parent, or friend.

2. Build Micro-Moments of Safety

- Use tone, posture, breath, silence, and validation to create space for others to show up.

3. Teach Remembering Practices

- Share journaling prompts, inner child work, breathwork, and golden rule reflections.

4. Create Remembering Spaces

- Host staff circles, community healing spaces, or group sessions where the aim isn't insight—but return.

MOVEMENTS THAT ALREADY EXIST

You are not alone.

- Trauma-informed systems (SAMHSA, 2014)
- Reflective supervision models (Emde & Wise, 2003)
- Narrative medicine and narrative therapy (White & Epston, 1990)
- Restorative justice frameworks
- Polyvagal-informed education and practice (Porges, 2011)
- Radical healing in BIPOC mental health movements (French et al., 2020)

Remembering is not new. It's ancient. We are just returning to what we've always known.

EXPERIENTIAL INSIGHT

You can lead a revolution quietly.

- In how you enter the room
- In how you say a name
- In how you pause instead of pathologize
- In how you see someone not for who they've become—but for who they still are beneath it all

That is how systems change. That is how legacies are rewritten. That is how the future is healed—one remembering at a time.

COMMITMENT PRACTICE

Today, I join the revolution of wholeness. I will not participate in forgetting. I will see people not through the lens of what broke them, but through the light of what remains. I will hold the mirror steady. I will return to myself again and again—and invite the world to do the same.

END-OF-CHAPTER SCIENTIFIC REFERENCES

- SAMHSA. (2014). Trauma-Informed Care in Behavioral Health Services (TIP 57).

- Emde, R. N., & Wise, B. K. (2003). Zero to Three Journal.

- White, M., & Epston, D. (1990). Narrative Means to Therapeutic Ends. Norton.

- Porges, S. W. (2011). The Polyvagal Theory. Norton.

- French, B. H., Lewis, J. A., Mosley, D. V., Adames, H. Y., Chavez-Dueñas, N. Y., Chen, G. A., & Neville, H. A. (2020). Toward a psychological framework of radical healing. The Counseling Psychologist, 48(1), 14–46.

Closing Poem: You Were Never Broken

You were not born to be fixed.

You were not made to be managed.

You were not designed for performance,

Nor survival disguised as success.

You were born

Curious.

Open.

Breathing fully.

Feeling deeply.

Trusting instinctively.

Before the silence.

Before the shame.

Before the script was handed to you

By those who had forgotten themselves.

And still—

Beneath the diagnosis,

Beneath the pattern,

Beneath the rage,

The resignation,

The ache to disappear—

You remained.

A pulse of truth.

A flicker of play.

A whisper of joy unafraid.

So now,

You do not need to become.

You only need to return.

Not to who you were told to be—

But to who you always were.

Not a fix.

Not a project.

But a remembering.

Not a healing.

But a homecoming.

Epilogue: You Were Always Enough

This is not a conclusion.

This is a recommitment.

Every morning, the forgetting begins again.

The world will try to sell you a self.

Systems will ask you to shrink.

The past will tempt you to identify with it.

Fear will wear the mask of logic.

Perfection will pose as purpose.

But you—

You now know the way back.

Back through breath.

Back through the body.

Back through the layers.

Back to presence.

Back to peace.

Back to the part of you that cannot be touched by trauma, titles, or time.

The pre-conditioned self never left.

It only waited for you to remember.

And now that you have—

Your presence becomes a doorway.

Your work becomes a mirror.

Your voice becomes an offering.

And in your remembering,

You become the light that helps others remember too.

You were always enough.

And now,

You are free to live like it.

Conclusion: From Remembering to Living

You've made the journey. From symptom to self. From fixing to remembering.

From the conditioned layers of pain to the quiet center of who you truly are.

You've moved through the four layers of transformation:

- You structured the conscious—where behavior and daily rhythms anchor safety.

- You explored the preconscious—where old beliefs and early schemas once ruled.

- You met the unconscious—where silence once held your forgotten truths.

- And you entered the existential—where you chose to live from freedom, not fear.

This book was never about information. It was about integration. It was never about fixing the mind. It was about freeing the self.

Now, as you step into the next chapter of your life, your work, your leadership, or your healing—remember this:

Healing is not a destination. Wholeness is not an achievement. Remembering is not something you do once. It's something you practice.

Every day you wake up and breathe with intention. Every time you pause instead of react. Every moment you choose compassion over control. Every time you look into someone's eyes and see their spark instead of their struggle—You are practicing remembering. And in that practice, you are not only healing yourself. You are healing the world. Because wholeness is contagious.

Where to Go From Here

- Use the tools. Print them. Share them. Teach them.

- Bring the four layers into your work, your teams, your sessions, your home.

- Let the pre-conditioned self speak a little louder every day.

- And when the forgetting returns—because it always does—return again. Gently. Without shame. You now know the path.

You Are the Model. You don't have to wait for permission. You don't need more credentials, more confidence, or a perfect plan. You only need your presence. Your presence is the practice.

Your presence is the medicine. Your presence is the invitation— for others to come home to themselves too. That is the work. That is the mission. That is the revolution. And it begins, again and again, with one simple, powerful truth:

You were never broken. You simply forgot. And now... you remember.

Invitation to You, the Reader

You've arrived at the end of this book, but not the end of your remembering. If something stirred in you…If you paused, cried, smiled, or softened… If a memory returned, or a part of you re-awakened…Then this book has already done its work.

But now it's your turn. This book is not meant to sit on a shelf. It is meant to live with you. In your breath. In your pauses. In your next decision. In the way you look at others—and yourself.

You are not just a reader. You are a remembering being.And the world needs more of us.

Reflection: A Question for You

Take a breath.

And ask yourself now:

What would change if I lived every day from the part of me that was never broken?

Write your answer.

Live your answer.

Let your answer become your legacy.

Your Call to Action

Here are 5 ways to continue your journey:

1. Practice the Tools

- Return to the 4 Layers. Use the Remembering Journal. Share the Golden Rule.

- Healing deepens through action.

2. Bring Remembering Into Your Work

- Whether you're a clinician, parent, educator, or leader—this model belongs in every system, every room, every relationship.

3. Host a Remembering Circle

- Gather your team. Invite your community. Start small. Ask: "What are we remembering together?"

4. Teach from This Book

5. Use the tools and practices in your groups, classrooms, or supervision. Cite the science. Honor the pre-conditioned self.

- Be the Mirror

Presence is powerful. Let the way you show up become someone else's remembering.

If This Book Moved You... If this book helped you see something new...If it reminded you of who you are...If it gave you language for something you've always known deep down...

Then please share it.

- Post a review online—your words help others find this work.
- Gift the book to someone navigating healing or burnout.
- Quote it in your work, your writing, your teaching.
- Email us your story—we would love to hear how remembering is showing up in your life.

Email: contact@sweetinstitute.com
Your story is part of the revolution.
Thank you for remembering with us.

With reverence,

Mardoche Sidor, MD
Karen Dubin, PhD, LCSW
SWEET Institute

Final Acknowledgments

As this book closes, our gratitude deepens. To the people we serve—You are not case numbers. You are not treatment plans. You are not the worst thing that ever happened to you.

You are whole. You are powerful. You are the reason we remember why we began.

Thank you for teaching us that healing is not always loud, not always linear, but always possible.

To the clinicians, case managers, supervisors, direct care staff, medical professionals, therapists, and support teams who show up—often under-resourced, under-recognized, and overburdened—thank you. Thank you for the way you hold space, even on hard days. Thank you for choosing to believe in the spark, not just the struggle.

To our mentors, teachers, and guides—seen and unseen—thank you for whispering wisdom when we needed it most.

To our ancestors, who remembered through oppression, war, migration, and silence—this book is your legacy too.

To our SWEET community—your brilliance, boldness, and integrity are woven into every word. You are building a new world with every breath, every choice, every question you ask out loud.

To our families—thank you for your patience and love as we poured our hearts into this work. You remind us what it means to be anchored in something real.

To everyone who carries this message forward:

You are part of something sacred.

You are not alone.

You are helping the world remember.

And for that,

We thank you.

With love and reverence,

Mardoche Sidor, MD

Karen Dubin, PhD, LCSW

SWEET Institute

The Reader Integration Toolkit

A Practical Guide to Moving from Insight to Implementation

This toolkit is your bridge—from remembering to living.

Use it as a daily practice, a weekly reflection, a therapeutic aid, or a compass during moments of confusion, reactivity, or forgetting. It is built to support sustained transformation across all four layers.

SECTION I: THE FOUR-LAYER DAILY SCAN

Use this once a day—or during moments of emotional overwhelm.

☰ THE FOUR-LAYER DAILY SCAN

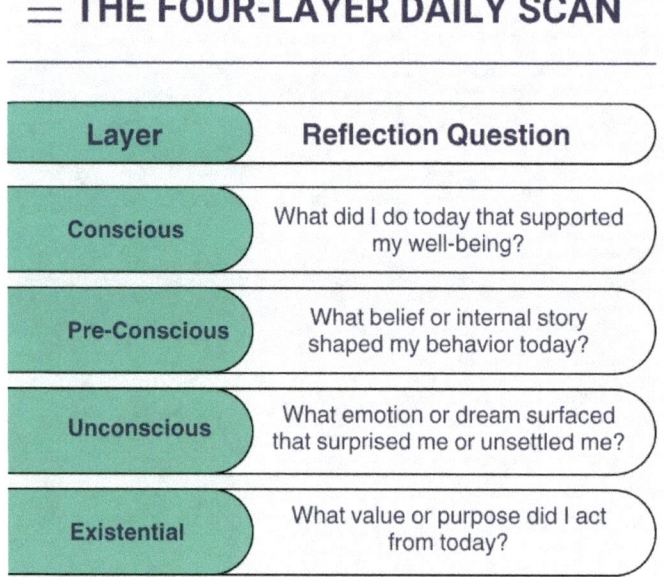

Layer	Reflection Question
Conscious	What did I do today that supported my well-being?
Pre-Conscious	What belief or internal story shaped my behavior today?
Unconscious	What emotion or dream surfaced that surprised me or unsettled me?
Existential	What value or purpose did I act from today?

Practice: Journal your responses daily for 21 days. Observe patterns, interruptions, and breakthroughs.

SECTION II: REMEMBERING PRACTICES

Morning Remembering Ritual (5–10 min)

- Breath: 3 deep inhales and exhales
- Say aloud:
    - "I was born whole. I am returning to myself."
    - Write down: One thing you want to remember about who you truly are today.

Evening Reflection Prompt

- What part of me showed up most today—my conditioned self or my pre-conditioned self?

SECTION III: SCHEMA MAPPING TOOL

Use this for uncovering preconscious patterns.

Step-by-Step:

1. Identify the situation that triggered you.
2. Notice the automatic thought or emotional reaction.
3. Ask: What core belief might be underneath this?
4. Trace it: Where did I first learn this?
5. Replace it: What would my pre-conditioned self say instead?

Example:

Trigger: A friend didn't text back.

Belief: "I'm being rejected."

Origin: Middle school bullying.

New message: "I am enough whether or not I receive constant reassurance."

SECTION IV: UNCONSCIOUS EXPLORATION TOOLS

Free Association Journal Prompt

Write without stopping for 3–5 minutes:

- "What I really want to say is…"

Let the unconscious speak. Don't edit. Then reread with curiosity.

Dream Tracker

Each morning, record:

- What happened
- How you felt
- Any symbols or standout images
- What associations come to mind
- One sentence the dream might be trying to tell you

SECTION V: EXISTENTIAL ALIGNMENT MAP

Weekly Alignment Exercise

1. What truly matters to me right now?
2. How did I live in alignment with that this week?
3. Where did I betray what matters to me?
4. What choice can I make this week to honor my freedom, purpose, or truth?

SECTION VI: INNER CHILD CHECK-IN

Do this at least once a week:

- Close your eyes. Visualize your 5–8 year-old self.
- Ask: What do you need from me right now?
- Respond out loud or in writing.

- Give yourself 5–10 minutes to offer what was requested: rest, play, reassurance, tears, laughter.

SECTION VII: GOLDEN RULE PRACTICE

Daily Check-In:

"Today, did I do for myself what I'd do for someone I love?"

Use this not as guilt—but as a gentle recalibration.

If not, ask:

What small act of remembering can I offer myself now?

SECTION VIII: INTEGRATION PLANNER

Use weekly to integrate all 4 layers.

≡ Integration Planner

Layer	This Week's Intention
Conscious	(Exercise, schedule, sleep, breathwork)
Pre-Conscious	(Identify belief, reframe inner dialogue)
Unconscious	(Track dreams, do one expressive writing session)
Existential	(Clarify value, practice the Golden Rule)

SECTION IX: SELF-CHECK FOR FORGETTING

When dysregulated, shut down, overwhelmed, or lost, pause and ask:

- What am I believing right now?
- Whose voice is this?
- What feeling am I avoiding?
- What would my pre-conditioned-self know right now?

Return. Breathe. Begin again.

SECTION X: YOUR REMEMBERING MANIFESTO

Write this. Print it. Post it. Live it.

I am not here to be fixed.

I am not a project. I am a presence.

I was born whole. I am returning to that truth daily.

I will not let systems define me, shame silence me, or fear shrink me.

I am remembering.

I am re-membering—rejoining the parts of me that were once exiled.

I will not forget again.

And when I do—I will return again.

Gently. Boldly. Fully.

Appendices

Appendix A:

THE FOUR LAYERS OF TRANSFORMATION – QUICK REFERENCE

Layer	Focus	Tools & Practices
Conscious	Behavior, habits, daily structure	Routine building, CBT tools, breathwork, sleep, nutrition, movement, scheduling
Preconscious	Schemas, beliefs, internal narratives	Schema mapping, ACT defusion, gestalt dialogue, inner child work
Unconscious	Repressed material, symbolic content	Free association, dream analysis, somatic awareness, projective writing
Existential	Meaning, freedom, purpose, identity	Values clarification, existential inquiry, Golden Rule practice, legacy reflection

Appendix B:

Core Schema Definitions (from Schema Therapy)

PROBLEM	DESCRIPTION
Abandonment	"People will leave me."
Mistrust/Abuse	"Others will hurt or use me."
Emotional Deprivation	"My needs will never be met."
Defectiveness/Shame	"Something is wrong with me."
Faillure	"I will never succeed."
Subjugation	"My needs and voice don't matter."
Unrelenting Standards	"I must always perform to be accepted."
Social Isolation	"I don't belong."

Use these schemas as an entry point in self-inquiry and therapeutic conversations.

Appendix C:

Golden Rule Daily Practice Prompts

- Did I treat myself as someone worthy of care today?
- Did I show compassion to someone else today without losing myself?
- Did I act in alignment with what I would want done unto me?
- Did I withhold something today (love, truth, forgiveness) out of fear or forgetting?

Use these questions in journaling, supervision, or team meetings.

Appendix D:

Language of Remembering (Words That Heal)

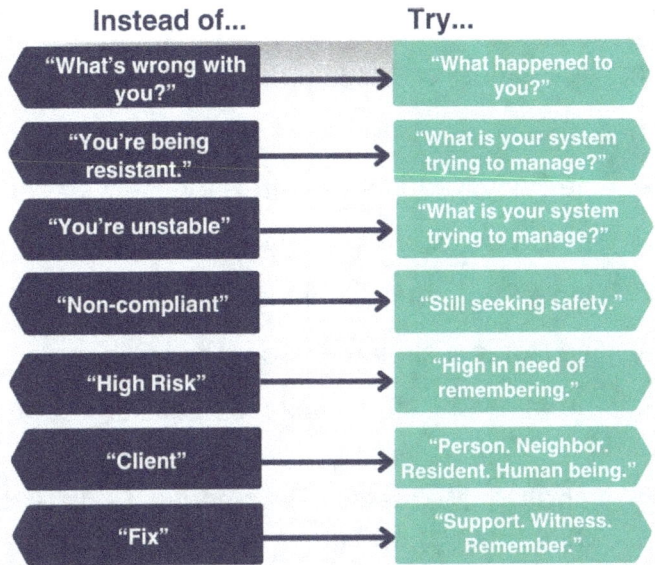

Instead of...	Try...
"What's wrong with you?"	"What happened to you?"
"You're being resistant."	"What is your system trying to manage?"
"You're unstable"	"What is your system trying to manage?"
"Non-compliant"	"Still seeking safety."
"High Risk"	"High in need of remembering."
"Client"	"Person. Neighbor. Resident. Human being."
"Fix"	"Support. Witness. Remember."

Language shapes consciousness. Let yours be an invitation.

Appendix E:

Daily Remembering Routine (Sample Template)

Morning (5 minutes)

- 3 mindful breaths
- Say: "I am returning to myself."
- Choose 1 intention (curiosity, softness, clarity)

Midday Pause

- Check: Am I living from fear, habit, or presence?
- Breathe. Return.

Evening Reflection

- What part of me led today?
- What did I remember?
- What will I carry forward into tomorrow?

Appendix F:

Suggested Resources for Continued Integration

Books:

- The Body Keeps the Score – Bessel van der Kolk
- The Developing Mind – Daniel J. Siegel
- Man's Search for Meaning – Viktor E. Frankl
- The Compassionate Mind – Paul Gilbert
- The Mindful Path to Self-Compassion – Christopher Germer
- Narrative Means to Therapeutic Ends – Michael White & David Epston

SWEET Institute Resources:

- SWEET Certificate Programs
- Motivational Interviewing & Schema Integration Courses
- Reflective Supervision Circles
- The SWEET Healing Circles
- www.sweetinstitute.com

Appendix G:

Facilitator's Quick Guide for Leading a Remembering Group

Group Goals:

- Support participants in accessing and sustaining the pre-conditioned self
- Integrate the four layers of transformation
- Build collective spaces of safety, choice, and dignity

Structure:

1. Opening Grounding Exercise (breath, silence, or reflection)
2. Group Check-in (Conscious & Preconscious layer scan)
3. Weekly Practice Focus (Schema Mapping, Existential Alignment)
4. Group Sharing (no fixing, only witnessing)
5. Closing Commitment

Group Agreements:

- Confidentiality
- No advice-giving
- Speak from the "I"
- Honor all parts of the self
- Practice returning—not perfection

Additional Resources by the Authors

To support your continued journey of remembering and integration, we invite you to explore the following books, trainings, and communities created by the authors.

Books by Mardoche Sidor, MD, and Karen Dubin, PhD, LCSW

- Before Anything Else, Validate (coming soon)
    - A practical and poetic guide to transforming relationships, leadership, and care through the power of validation.

- The Courage to Care: Stories of Healing, Hope, and the Power of Social Work
    - A collection of narratives from frontline clinicians that redefines the heart of the helping professions.

- Breaking the Pattern: (Coming soon)
    - Understanding and Healing Repetition Compulsion
    - A layered, scientific, and experiential approach to ending cycles of trauma and self-sabotage.

- How Life Works (Coming soon)
    - A transformational guide to understanding life's lessons, reclaiming personal power, and choosing healing over habit.

- The Simplicity Principle (Coming soon)
    - A practical framework for mastering learning, growth, and clarity by breaking everything down into what matters most.

- Freeing Fear (Coming soon)
  - A journey through the conscious, preconscious, and unconscious roots of fear—and the path to freedom.
- The Kindness Imperative (Coming soon)
  - A guide to power, purpose, and true leadership—built on the science and spirituality of radical kindness.
- The Still Point (Coming soon)
  - A meditative, narrative-based exploration of presence, purpose, and the quiet revolution of self-awareness.
- Rewriting the Script (Coming soon)
  - A transformational guide to healing internalized oppression through the power of narrative and community.
- For the complete and growing list of titles, visit:
  - www.SWEETInstitutePublishing.com

SWEET Institute Training and Certificate Programs

- The 4 Layers of Transformation Certificate
  - A comprehensive course on the Conscious, Preconscious, Unconscious, and Existential levels of change.
- Motivational Interviewing, Schema Work, and Behavior Change
  - Training designed to help you implement real-time clinical change across diverse systems.
- SWEET Healing Circles
  - Join guided, experiential spaces for remembering, integration, and community-based healing.

- Leadership for Mental Health and Social Service Professionals
  - A layered model of time mastery, accountability, and presence-based leadership.

Visit www.SWEETInstitute.com for course schedules, memberships, and community access.

Connect With Us

- Email: contact@sweetinstitute.com
- LinkedIn: SWEET Institute
- YouTube: SWEET Institute Channel
- Podcast: The Remembering Revolution (coming soon)

You are not alone on this journey.

Join the movement.
Be part of the remembering.

About the Authors

Mardoche Sidor, MD

Dr. Mardoche Sidor is a Harvard- and Columbia-trained, quadruple-board-certified psychiatrist with subspecialties in Child and Adolescent Psychiatry, Forensic Psychiatry, Addiction Psychiatry, and Public/Community Psychiatry. He has also trained in Geriatric Psychiatry and is widely known for bridging cutting-edge science with deep clinical wisdom.

Dr. Sidor is the founder of the SWEET Institute, where he leads transformative education for clinicians, leaders, and human service professionals. He previously served as Assistant Clinical Professor of Psychiatry at Columbia University-Vagelos School of Physicians and Surgeons, for eight years and currently serves as Medical Director at Urban Pathways in New York City.

Through his teaching, books, and leadership, Dr. Sidor invites others into a new model of care—one rooted not in fixing, but in remembering. He believes that true healing begins when people return to who they were before the conditioning, and that clinicians and systems can evolve to reflect this truth.

Karen Dubin, PhD, LCSW

Dr. Karen Dubin is a clinical social worker, educator, and writer with almost three decades of experience at the intersection of trauma healing, systems change, and clinical supervision. She holds a PhD in Social Work and a master's in both clinical practice and education, with advanced training in solution-focused therapy, narrative therapy, and adult learning.

As the Director of Learning at the SWEET Institute, Dr. Dubin helps lead a national movement of remembering-based care, guiding clinicians across the country in the art and science of deep, sustainable transformation.

She is known for her ability to bring humanity, humor, and clarity to even the most complex challenges in mental health and human services. Her work, writing, and presence remind us that our greatest power lies not in what we know—but in how we show up.

Together, Dr. Sidor and Dr. Dubin co-lead the SWEET Institute Publishing platform, offering books, training, and tools that advance a new paradigm of healing—one rooted in integration, wholeness, and the sacred art of remembering.

To learn more or connect with the authors:

www.SWEETInstitute.com
www.SWEETInstitutePublishing.com

www.ingramcontent.com/pod-product-compliance
Lightning Source LLC
Chambersburg PA
CBHW071206120626
46546CB00006B/2447